Keep Your Feet Moving And Navigate Challenges On The Way To Entrepreneurship

CYNDI MCCOY

Published by TEOT Press

Cover design Rob Williams

ISBN: 978-1-7327452-1-6

DEDICATION

This book is dedicated to the seekers, action takers, and go-getters, everyday people who summon the courage to get unstuck and build bridges beyond their circumstances that transform their lives and the lives of others.

CONTENTS

"THE ONLY COURAGE YOU EVER NEED IS THE COURAGE TO FULFILL THE DREAMS OF YOUR OWN LIFE."
-OPRAH WINFREY

ACKNOWLEDGMENTS

De, I am blessed to have you in my life and appreciate all you do.

Charles your wisdom amazes me, thank you for your understanding and support.

Sam Wright, my editor without you my words would still be scattered on pages.

Kaylee Robinson and Gail Seymour this could not happen without your hard work. I honestly do not know what I would do without you.

Sandra Herndon, Patricia Davis, and Tonya Moore thank you for your feedback.

To the Downtown Dallas Women's Entrepreneur group, Nicole Robinson, Jennifer Conner, and Lori Miller thank you for keeping me on track.

To The Firewheel Fictionistas Writers Group, Brian Wells, Maggie Foster, Mary Herrera, I am humbled and grateful for your guidance and support.

To my coaches, Lisa Nichols and Tiana Von Johnson every one of your comments and suggestions were received and implemented with gratitude. This book would not be possible without your impressive genius.

To my clients, Thank you for giving me the greatest gift of all your trust. Helping you succeed is one of my greatest pleasures.

To the reader... Thank you for reading this book and making the commitment to build a bridge to the life you were always meant to live.

If you like, the book let us know on Facebook at the following
www.facebook.com/groups/KeepYourFeetMoving/

INTRODUCTION

If you faced several 250-pound linebackers hell-bent on clobbering you, your best bet is to keep your feet moving. Otherwise, you might become food for the astroturf. "Keep your feet moving" is a coaching metaphor often used in football to train receivers and running backs not to stop when running the ball.

Just as in football, obstacles can stop anyone from plowing forward in life, from reaching their goal. If a running back can keep moving, their chance of navigating a pile-up dramatically increases. If the same athlete does not continue running through the pile of players, he could end up stuck. Many people feel chained in their lives and not sure how to break free and move their feet again.

The ability to keep moving, despite challenges, increases the chances of coming out of the situation. We think what we go through daily happens only to us. When discouragement, pessimism, and exhaustion creep in, we feel like a hostage in our own life. We desperately look for an escape route but keep hitting a wall of challenges. Similar to a movie, that keeps playing the same scene, words, and actions in a seemingly never-ending circle.

Does this sound familiar? Your day starts as it has for years, with the alarm clock sounding. With a deep sigh, you drag yourself out of bed to begin juggling all your personal, financial, and professional responsibilities. As you desperately try to keep all the plates in the air, a nagging feeling makes you wonder, "Is this all?

"Have you ever worked at a job you outgrew, leaving you

desperately wanting a different career?

The new career required an advanced degree, years of experience, or a contact in the industry. You can do the work but do not have time, money, or network to break into a new industry. So, you stay bound to a job that does not maximize your talents and skills.

By chance, maybe you are the breadwinner but shouldering all the decisions has caused stress and insomnia while contributing to a host of medical problems. Perhaps there is more month than money left over. Demands pulling you in so many directions your outgoing personality and focus have given way to forgetfulness and burnout. Maybe you care for others with no acknowledgment for your sacrifice and think, when is it my turn to dream?

Imagine having a dream to start a business, buy a home, pursue a college degree, write a book, or adopt a wellness lifestyle. You save the money that will transform your life financially when an immediate repair, family member, friend, or emergency requires the money.

When stuck, we see no way out, even though there are solutions. The remedy may require a plan to reframe thoughts, and actions to get unstuck. The resolution may need self-care, nutritional, functional, clinical, or behavioral support. Consult professionals for the appropriate diagnosis and treatment.

This book provides a self-care framework to navigate the rollercoaster of thinking, relationships, and actions that challenge our dreams of a better life. Expressly, to navigate the rollercoaster of life before the barrage of challenges and setbacks lead to the state of addiction or detrimental mental health outcomes.

KEEP YOUR FEET MOVING AND NAVIGATE CHALLENGES
ON THE ROAD TO ENTREPRENEURSHIP

You are probably wondering about my own experiences with challenges. I am not the exception I have been stuck often in life and business. I married and flew to a new metropolis with a spouse and no family or friends. I could not find work, dug my way out of a melancholic state, and later started my first business acquiring and managing real estate. The stress contributed to weight gain and hormonal fluctuations. Then years later, starting a second business helping entrepreneurs and Fortune 500 companies create new products and build businesses.

This book will keep your feet moving using an adaptable plan to help you navigate the challenges of life by moving past fear and overwhelm. It is time to dream again.

The lessons learned are from years of consulting work with clients and businesses from the information technology, telecom, healthcare, financial services, retail, and government industries. Besides, the process of locating a doctor that takes a holistic approach to address issues caused by stress, and the rollercoaster of highs and lows from relocating every few years, to developing new relationships, and starting new businesses. I intend to save you time and frustration, so you do not make the same mistakes.

We will discuss in the following chapters circumstances contributing to feeling stuck and how to use The Shift, Download, and Propel roadmap to build a bridge from limiting thoughts and actions that derail our dreams to desires of a better life and business.

"WHEN I LET GO OF WHAT I AM, I BECOME WHAT I MIGHT BE"
-LAO TZU

CHAPTER 1: AM I STUCK?

Have you ever downloaded an application for your Smartphone and as you were waiting for the download to finish, the status bar stopped moving?

Have you ever rented a DVD or streamed a movie and during the best part of the film, the same scene kept replaying over and over?

The downloaded application and the movie were stuck, and before either would move, you had to do something to help them get unstuck. One way being stuck manifests in life is our pattern of thinking. I moved to a new city with my spouse and expected the interview and hiring process to be like my previous experiences. I did not change the approach that always got me hired, even when the method stopped working.

My fixed thoughts were evident in my actions when my doctor recommended a reduction in weight. I agreed and after going to the gym, continued to eat my favorite pasta and bread only to be confused by the weigh-in scale. Stuck was also evident in my view of the world, I saw the world as a limited cold, and cruel place. It never occurred that I was stuck in a pattern of thinking and acting.

Sometimes we perform day-to-day responsibilities feeling paralyzed, wanting to change, but not knowing what to do. Have you ever went through the day and not even remembered driving to work it is like you were on autopilot and not even realizing you are stuck? I knew I was stuck when the usual coping mechanisms of watching TV, eating, shopping, and partying no longer brought relief from the dull ache of living.

Careers and relationships no longer provided joy or satisfaction and routine tasks became difficult to manage. We sometimes hit a wall when deep inside we know we are not using our talents. It is easier to stay in the comfort of routine and ignore the inner prompting and ache of unhappiness.

Why am I stuck?

According to neuroscientist Dr. Joe Dispenza's Breaking the Habit of Being Yourself, the brain takes a picture of emotional experiences rehearsed repeatedly. The practice of repeating events, circumstances, and situations.

both silently and aloud signals the mind this is important. Thinking can cue a rush of emotions so frequently that the body gets used to the feeling and labels it as normal.

Once the mind has built a connection between the trigger of bills, recruiters, and managers' words, the mind constructs a road. The brain uses the pathway the next time an event happens that reminds you of the emotional experience, so the event triggers the thought, thinking triggers an emotion, the emotion triggers words, and the cycle continues until a belief forms.

After living in the Midwest for most of my life, our family moved to the Southwest. The first few months in our new state it rained and was bone chilling cold...Still, I was anxious to make friends and find work. My self-confidence swelled after quickly securing several interviews.

 The hiring manager looked at me with eyebrows pulled down and nose wrinkled and asked, "Did you attend university on campus or online?" Eyes wide open; I studied his face, leaned forward, and explained that I attended both online and on campus because my work schedule required frequent travel to locations in different states.

"Why didn't you attend an accredited university?" After recovering from my initial disbelief, I explained the University of Phoenix is an accredited university recognized by the Department of Education and the Council for Higher Education Accreditation. "Well, we won't train you for the job," he said. Setting up straight in the chair while smiling, I shared a brief summary of the business results from a decade of experience.

How education combined with a technical background and rising through the ranks to leadership combined with emotional intelligence made me a perfect fit for the position and culture.

"We will call you, goodbye." This scenario played out repeatedly with recruiters and hiring managers, I became skilled at preparing rebuttals for every objection. Still, my replies fell on deaf ears as dismissals and failure became the norm. My words grew increasingly hypercritical as self-doubt reared its monstrous head. I felt the energy leave my body every time the mail arrived. Three months, six months, twelve months, no work, disappointment, shame, and doubt all triggered by the uncertainty of a new environment.

The route in my brain formed as I began believing recruiters and hiring managers' words. I even questioned prior successes and present abilities.

Doubts keep us stuck, especially when dealing with the discomfort of unemployment. This unknown kept me from moving forward and quickly turned into fear. A hurricane or other natural disaster triggers fear and prompts the body to leave the area.

Doubt gave way to paralyzing fear. I kept reflecting on the problems instead of searching for solutions. Has fear ever prevented you from making better decisions for your life?

"MAY YOUR CHOICES REFLECT
YOUR HOPES, NOT YOUR FEARS"
- NELSON MANDELA

SHIFT

/SHIFT/

[MERRIAM-WEBSTER DICTIONARY]

VERB

TO STOP GOING IN ONE DIRECTION
AND/OR CHANGE POSITIONS

NOUN

TO TURN AWAY FROM AND/OR
MOVE IN A DIFFERENT DIRECTION

HE MADE A DECISION TO STOP
MAKING EXCUSES FOR LIFE AND
STARTED LOOKING FOR THE
SOLUTIONS TO PROBLEMS.

CHAPTER 2: THE SHIFT

It was an unenthused spring day in the Midwest. "Yes, I will marry you," I said to De on bended knee with a ring in hand. My heart was pounding, and the first thought was, what did I do?

While I said 'yes' to De's proposal, I additionally said,
Yes to leaving the only home, I ever knew.
Yes to moving away from my family, job, childhood,
 and college friends

How would this decision change my life? I would have to find a place to live, make new friends, and find meaningful work.

Let us return to another job interview.

Heart pounding and short breaths paved the way for a full panic attack, as I called recruiters, managers, and networked all while enduring failure after failure. Internally, I was continually repeating the words and actions of hiring managers during many interviews, "You did not go to a real college," and "How do we know this degree is real?"

Many had a limited view and believed if you did not attend college on campus, that you did not go to a real university. This was during the late 1990's when the internet exploded on to the scene. By the year 2010, "the Sloan Asynchronous Learning Network estimates nearly three million students enrolled in online degree programs for which 70% attended for-profit universities.

"Today, many employers value candidates' dedication to

education. They understand the resiliency, time management, and collaboration required balancing a full-time job and family to obtain an education. Of course, the perception varies depending on the company.

My planning and efforts to learn about businesses, industries, and networking did not change the outcome. My replies to hiring managers' objections were unfruitful. I am typically a confident, hard-working believer who tithes, but as time passed, lack of confidence set in as my hard work was not rewarded.

The commercials promising bankruptcy seemed the only answer. Yes, it was that bad! I was in the midst of losing material things that seemed relevant. The constant focus on my problems and feelings caused me to sink into a deep malaise.

It felt very much like my life had dried up and withered away like leaves on dead trees. Is this all life has for me? I was beginning to give up.

Have negative thoughts ever swirled around your head as you focused on the cause of your pain, instead of what the pain may be telling you?

One-day while channel surfing, I stumbled upon an inspirational program by Bishop T. D. Jakes. He discussed his book; Reposition Yourself, Living Life without Limits. He talked about hurricane Katrina and Rita survivors, and Oceanic survivors of flight 815. He increased the message to include anyone fighting to get from one place to another position.

The survivors were stuck and wondering if they would

ever get out. The hurricane and crash confused their internal

navigation systems. The first question they asked was, "Where am I and how do I get out?" The message spoke to my situation. The crash of recruiters and hiring managers' words and actions confused my internal perspective. The constant conflict of views caused my navigation to move off course.

T. D. Jakes program motivated me to focus on what was left and not what was lost. This shift in perspective introduced me face-to-face with my limited mindset and its impact on my feelings and actions.

After the interview failures, I did not know what to do, but was determined to find a solution and began writing down work results, history, and talents. Writing down my work and results is the first of many steps to answer the 'where am I' question. The next step is to solve the problem of "how do I get out?"

Once the shift in focus started, my mindset had to be reprogrammed to interpret and respond to situations differently. Dr. Carol Dweck's book, Mindset, The New Psychology of Success, presupposes "every situation and circumstance resulting from our environment is stored mentally. As experiences repeat over time, the mind develops pathways to connect the experiences." This suggests our environment reinforces past learned actions, thoughts, and beliefs.

Dr. Dweck talks about how the fixed and growth mindsets have recognizable patterns, especially with failure. The fixed mindset feels smart and talented only when making no mistakes and quickly completing assignments.

The growth mindset views mistakes as a challenge and tries

to learn to become better at completing tasks.

Her book helped me to understand how limited beliefs affected my thoughts, feelings, and relationships. I needed to change my limited mindset before my situation would improve.

The next steps were to take a sheet of paper and create three columns. In one column, including the skills, people, and assets that are left, the middle column, include your dreams for the future. For the third column, write down, what you need to learn to make the future a reality. As I read over the list, the items in the first column made me feel grateful, and the things in the middle column helped me to visualize the future.

The first baby steps began with reading books and attending workshops. This increased working knowledge and changed my belief system. What thoughts do I need to change?

During the reading of many health books, I learned to use the breath as a tool to calm emotions and reduce stress. That cardio and strength training produce new brain cells. The next step was to incorporate daily exercise. I walked around the lake and listened to the sounds of birds and the wind. Over time, this practice helped to clear my mind and caused me to focus on the visions written in the future column.

The stress of needing a paycheck for monthly bills clouded the ability to think. I was stuck in a pattern of thinking, acting, and engaging with people. Anxiety and desperation kept my focus on the obstacles and setbacks to survival. "Will I lose the house?" and "will my relationships last without money?" T.D. Jakes's book Reposition Yourself talked about how you always have something left and to use whatever is in your hands.

I focused on the innovations and improvements my work

provided for different companies instead of responses from hiring managers and recruiters. The changes were for new technology products and services that never existed in the past. The improvements were for existing systems and processes that were re-engineered to provide additional cost savings for those companies.

When I took inventory of my business results and focused on what was in my hands, a new sense of energy emerged with the thought, I can do this!

I have experienced many technological revolutions since the 1990's. McAfee and Brynjolfsson's Machine, Platform, Crowd talks about the impact of the Internet of Things, Artificial Intelligence, 3-D printing, autonomous vehicles, Biotechnology, and Nanotechnology will have on productivity and the quality of life. Technology and the innovation economy offer us great opportunities, but the key to thriving in the innovation economy is entrepreneurship. This means there are opportunities to create solutions to the challenges of our world.

The problem required a shift in perspective. The resulting pain pushed me to focus on a solution. Who knew the resolution to the problem would be entrepreneurship?

I was willing to do anything, even if that meant changing my thoughts, obtaining new knowledge, and seeking different people. My limited mindset was useful for managing the traditional operations of a career. The value provided to organizations was significant. If recruiters and hiring managers could not see the value, others would see and want the benefits.

I called a contact at a Fortune 500 company and pitched them my services. "Hi, what can you do for us?" said Mike.

I provided leadership for large cross-functional business-to-business teams for new next generation technology used for automation. Then for another company, created a hybrid development lifecycle to re-engineer product delivery in three weeks instead of the typical six months. For a startup, developed and presented a strategy to improve efficiency and saved millions of dollars.

Mike transferred me to the vendor supply department to complete paperwork to bid on the business offered to third-party vendors. Months later, congratulations you won the bid, this was music to my ears!

I accepted the risk of charting my own course and started adapting the growth mindset of an entrepreneur. Have you ever wanted to change your finances, relationships, career, or health, but did not know where to start, what to do, or have the support of family or friends?

KEEP YOUR FEET MOVING AND NAVIGATE CHALLENGES
ON THE ROAD TO ENTREPRENEURSHIP

THE SHIFT LESSONS LEARNED

1) Practice gratitude - every day write in your planner or journal three things you are most thankful.

2) Exercise - incorporate daily practice for 10-15 minutes and increase as fitness improves. Search YouTube for beginner exercises, yoga, and low-impact cardio. Select a 5 to 10-minute video; add it to your playlist. Then, set a calendar reminder to exercise three times a week, for example, Monday, Wednesday, and Friday.

3) Visualize your future - close your eyes and imagine yourself in a movie with your favorite movie star. Where would you live, would the weather be sunny, snowy, or raining? What type of house would you live in, what kind of friends would you invite over for dinner?
What work would bring a smile to your face?

4) Inventory your talents - take Tom Rath's Strength finders 2.0 test as a starting point to discover your top five talents.

5) Create a list of your talents - in your planner or journal create three columns, one with the abilities you have now, the second from your visualization, and the third column, what you need to learn for your future.

This small shift of implementing the lessons learned will lead to another step, downloading new information to find direction. The next chapter will talk about the importance of downloading data. Seeking further information is an essential step to transition the mindset, relationships, and actions required to propel you toward those dreams.

PRACTICE THE SHIFT LESSONS LEARNED EXERCISE IN THE APPENDIX

DOWNLOAD

/DOUNLŌD/

[MERRIAM WEBSTER DICTIONARY]

VERB

COPY DATA FROM ONE COMPUTER
SYSTEM TO ANOTHER SYSTEM

NOUN

THE ACT OR PROCESS OF
DOWNLOADING DATA, KNOWLEDGE,
INFORMATION, AND
UNDERSTANDING.

GET INFORMATION, KNOWLEDGE,
AND UNDERSTANDING BY
WATCHING, READING, LISTENING,
AND PRACTICING FROM OTHERS.

CHAPTER 3: DOWNLOAD

There are many ways to acquire information, whether downloading applications, taking online classes, learning from other entrepreneurs, mothers, fathers, and professionals. Reading, podcasts, workshops, coaches, mastermind groups, and traveling are lovely ways to acquire information.

It takes time, and effort to acquire new information, and you may encounter many of the same setbacks in increasing your working knowledge that contributed to being stuck. Thoughts, such as I have to do laundry, cook or forgot to pay a bill or the last-minute fire drills for assistance from, coworkers, friends, and family.

We do not want to neglect obligations but need the alone time to acquire new knowledge to propel toward our dreams. Your child asks for help with homework and the next thing, you are loading the dishwasher, and picking up around the house. It is bedtime and did not have time to work on that business idea.

Doing the same thing, the same way, around the same people for too long becomes comfortable and before you know...we are stuck. Family and friends begin to question if you can start a business, move up the career ladder, get a degree, or lose weight. Self-doubt creeps in as you wonder if you can do this.

Do you really want to do this? Is your health, business, or career important?

How important is this on a scale of one to 10?
 If this dream ranks number one, then hard decisions are

required to carve out time and resources. This is where the lessons learned from Keep Your Feet moving can help to form a flexible plan to move through obstacles and challenges.

The plan is to shift time from what you are doing and use that time to focus on working toward dreams and goals. Download the information and data based on the results of your inventory, visualization, and future list.

One new thing learned, provides the mind with advanced information, and is a part of the process to upgrade the mindset, relationships, and actions. These areas require an upgrade to propel you in a new direction.

"YOUR BELIEFS BECOME YOUR
THOUGHTS, YOUR THOUGHTS
BECOME YOUR WORDS, YOUR
WORDS BECOME YOUR ACTIONS,
YOUR ACTIONS BECOME YOUR
HABITS, YOUR HABITS BECOME
YOUR VALUES, AND YOUR VALUES
BECOME YOUR DESTINY."
- MAHATMA GANDHI

CHAPTER 4: MINDSET

Everything created started in the brain; look at your clothing. The shirt or dress began in the designer's mind before she or he put the design on the material.

The house, condominium, apartment, or building you live in were first thoughts in the architect's mind before he or she created the blueprint. The mobile device, electronics, and the light bulb started as ideas in the inventor's mind. Your mindset determines how you see yourself. Stanford University Psychologist, Dr. Carol Dweck discovered Fixed and Growth Mindset, the premise that mindsets are the words, thoughts, feelings, and understanding of your intelligence, skills, and actions.

When I was interviewing with recruiters and hiring managers, my research of the industry, business, and work results informed my responses of how my skills and experience solved the problem the position was to resolve. A fixed mindset clouds judgment and robs us of the ability to use critical thinking skills.

Dr. Dweck suggests adopting a growth mindset to improve capacity by considering that intelligence is not limited but expands with effort and practice.

I engaged with different people and spent time with other entrepreneurs, business owners, and coaches. They inspired and motivated me to start a business and shared tips on how to succeed. Had I continued operating in the fixed mindset, I would have never believed the possibility of starting a business or helping other entrepreneurs grow their businesses.

Belief and unbelief often cohabitate, we often believe we can increase knowledge to move up the career ladder but do not think we have enough intelligence to start a business or become an entrepreneur.

If others see your potential, but you have a fixed mindset, your belief will cause you to ignore their recommendations. Create a daily routine to incorporate new information by asking, what can I do differently and who can help me get started?

Thought leaders and entrepreneurs think we are living in a time of unprecedented change. History reveals many businesses did not transform from one cycle of innovation to the next; Dr. Dweck's research suggests mindset plays a significant role in the failure.

Mindset is crucial because it is the determining factor in how we respond to the challenges and setbacks of life. We react to failure with the belief we are powerless or can learn to increase our abilities. This research shows the mind responds to learning new things as muscle capacity expands with exercise.

Small changes in thinking can create significant changes in what we do every day and make a big difference in achieving dreams.

MINDSET LESSONS LEARNED

1) Invest in learning about yourself - spend time learning about your talents, abilities, and temperament.

2) Increase your knowledge base - reading and engaging with topics that excite curiosity.

3) Physical activity - experiment with the timing of exercise, do you get different thoughts, emotions, and physical responses when you do not exercise before obtaining knowledge? Are there any differences when you download on an empty versus a full stomach?

4) Awareness - notice patterns of thought, emotions, and physical responses that surface as you incorporate new downloads into your daily practice. Are you focused and energized as you stretch beyond comfort zones or are negative thoughts running in a loop telling you it will never work and asking you to give up?

5) Practice mindfulness, meditation, or deep breathing - start with 5 minutes breathing in through the nose and out through the mouth. This will calm the mind and if negative thoughts are playing in your head do not resist the thinking just note the logic.

It takes effort and time to reprogram years of learned beliefs. We accept mistakes are part of the process. Want to start a business, adopt a healthier lifestyle, or go after that promotion, forgive others and yourself then keep your feet moving to get back on track.

PRACTICE MINDSET LESSONS LEARNED EXERCISE IN THE APPENDIX

"THERE ARE NO NEUTRAL RELATIONSHIPS. EACH ONE LIFTS YOU UP OR WEIGHS YOU DOWN; IT MOVES YOU FORWARD OR HOLDS YOU BACK." - THE PEOPLE FACTOR, -VAN MOODY

KEEP YOUR FEET MOVING AND NAVIGATE CHALLENGES ON THE ROAD TO ENTREPRENEURSHIP

CHAPTER 5: RELATIONSHIPS

Relationships have many definitions depending on the type. A contact can be that of a family member. A tie can be a friend you share similar backgrounds. The connection can be warm and energetic like a love interest.

We typically choose relationships based on commonality or happenstance due to work, travel, or other circumstances. Relationships often form because you have something the other wants to obtain.

I was stuck in a pattern of engaging with the same people, acting the same way over, and over for years. Until I implemented new knowledge downloads and joined different groups. Through interaction with other courageous men and women from different races, religions, socio-economic status, and political affiliations, many of whom shared pain and lessons learned.

These beautiful people shared their stories of starting businesses, birthing children, obtaining college degrees, writing books, burying loved ones, and overcoming illness. The type and quality of relationships have an intense effect on life and business.

The encouragement, hugs, and tears gave me support to pursue my dream of entrepreneurship. A growth mindset chooses relationships that honor and brings out our best. This practice takes time as our values grow and deepen in correlation to our understanding of ourselves.

Relationships that dishonor
Smiles in your face but undermines you to others.

Does not share information but asks you to provide

information.

Does not honor promises or provide updates for missed commitments.

Relationships that honor

Is transparent, tells you the truth no matter how painful.

Shares information and best practices for win-win strategies.

Honors promises and missed commitments are exceptions and not the rule.

Social Networks makes it easier to connect with casual followers. Why do others follow you on Social Media, is this because you are sharing information that benefits them? When the times reverse, and you need something, will followers be available to you? A one-sided relationship can cause psychological damage and impair future relationship decisions.

Relationships can be of a transactional nature such as a business partner, employer, and employee or non-transactional. Regardless of the affiliation, make sure you are both on the same page on the type of relationship-- transactional, non-transactional, or a hybrid of the two.

 Relationships are meaningful because of the human need to connect with others on a deeper level. Here are lessons learned to help you choose relationships that honor and bring out the best in you.

RELATIONSHIP LESSONS LEARNED

1) Assemble your team of supporters - go on the hunt and build relationships with people who will support you and propel you toward those dreams. Seek people that are genuine have achieved similar goals and will share their

knowledge and wisdom. This is an essential step toward attaining any dream.

2) Surround yourself - with people who benefit you as much as you help them - Conduct research and network with a purpose to build authentic relationships that appreciate and make room for you in their life.

3) Convenience - do not allow comfort or convenience to prevent you from deepening relationships that encourage your future. Relationships require work but can multiple your life and add value.

4) Eat the meat - do not take rejection or criticism from others as a personal attack, think of it as food, eat the flesh, and throw away the bones.

5) Forgive yourself and others - release disappointment and anger toward others and yourself, especially when those relationships encourage thinking and behaviors that do not serve your future.

We all make mistakes and it takes time to learn who to listen and not listen to and if they are family or coworkers, limit time spent engaging with them. Make cultivating the right relationships a priority.

PRACTICE RELATIONSHIP LESSONS LEARNED EXERCISE IN THE APPENDIX

VISHEN LAKHIANI, "THE CODE OF THE EXTRAORDINARY MIND, INTRODUCES THE CONCEPT OF CONSCIOUS ENGINEERING, THE PREMISE IS GROWTH DEPENDS ON REWRITING YOUR MODEL OF REALITY AND UPGRADING YOUR SYSTEMS FOR LIVING."

CHAPTER 6: ACTIONS

We often flirt with our dreams thinking about them, watching others from the sidelines, attending seminars and conferences, hoping and waiting for the desire to knock on the door.

You may have taken action and obtained business cards, a website, and let people know you offer a product or service. These actions may provide some income but your business is not growing, and you want to go to the next level.

You may have started exercising and following an eating plan to help lose weight and move toward living a healthier lifestyle. A life event, emotional setback, or challenge has you reaching for a sugar fix. Upon review of your career accomplishments and tenure, you decide to apply for the promotion. The director chooses someone with less experience and achievements. When you ask what you could do better next time, his vague answer confuses you.

Think of the above situations as you would a vacation to a dream locale. Thumbing through pages on a website, viewing pictures of the landscape and sitting by the water with the wind blowing seems like paradise. We make the decision to go on a dream vacation and need to build a bridge to help us get from we are to the place we can see.

Planning a vacation would mean researching airline and hotel prices along with dates for the best rates. Once the time for travel is set, begin strategizing on how to save money for the vacation. We talk about the upcoming trip with others to inspire and motivate actions. We decided to pack lunch for work, cook dinner, and watch movies at home, and put those savings toward the trip.

You effectively built a bridge from the present situation to the future dream. Setbacks can devastate the most resilient, often leaving a significant gap between you and the goal you want.

I created Keep Your Feet Moving as a bridge to help me close the distance from my current circumstances to the dream on the other side. Research has shown the number one obstacle preventing people from pursuing their dreams is fear. The heart pounding cannot breathe emotional hell that paralyzes our brain so we cannot think or act. Use what you are running from or to as fuel for action.

When you act, it shows your mind and others,
I take responsibility for the outcome of my life.
I will not wait at the elevator for my dreams to come true.
I will take the stairs. I will learn what I need to learn.

Taking action is one of the most critical steps in the Shift, Download, and Propel chapters, without acting I never would have found my mission, to help people become entrepreneurs so they can participate in the innovation economy.

ACTIONS LESSONS LEARNED

1) Change the information - seek knowledge and ask questions to obtain answers and identify what to read, listen, and watch to support your dreams. Study daily for a minimum of 5 hours a week.

2) Change how you talk - you can do more than you think ... you can have that business, promotion, healthy lifestyle,

etc.

When negative thoughts such as anger and resentment surface use Dr. Mercola's Emotional Freedom Technique to release emotions. Do not allow feelings to make your decisions. You can do this!

3) Get out of your comfort zone - every week reach out and connect with someone who has obtained or is pursuing your dream. Do something that you have wanted to do but have been afraid.

4) Set up boundaries, order, and structure - use the lessons learned from Keep Your Feet Moving as a flexible plan to get back on track when thoughts, relationships, and actions derail goals.

5) Evaluate conflicting and different types of data - It takes a combination of education, life experiences, emotional intelligence, intuition, and trial and error to evaluate data. There are always tradeoffs, for example, listen carefully to commercials telling you about medicines as with any information always look for the pros and cons of information in the evaluation of data.

Practice, practice, practice incorporating the action lessons learned in your daily routine until it becomes a habit.

PRACTICE ACTIONS LESSONS LEARNED EXERCISE IN THE APPENDIX

CYNDI MCCOY

PROPEL

/PRƏ'PEL/

[MERRIAM WEBSTER DICTIONARY]

VERB

TO DRIVE, PUSH, OR CAUSE TO
MOVE, TYPICALLY FORWARD.

SHE STARTED A BUSINESS AND
PROPELLED IT FORWARD USING
DOWNLOADS GLEANED FROM
OTHERS.

FEAR PROPELLED HER OUT OF HER
STILLNESS.

CHAPTER 7: PROPEL

The America Ninja Warrior Television™ show features competitors attempting to complete obstacle courses, each with increasing difficulty hoping to become the next American Ninja Warrior and winning the prize.

Many of the show's competitors encounter disappointments and failures that sideline their goals, but others go on to the finals. Competitors going through the demanding course must throw themselves forward to reach the next obstacle while the clock ticks away.

We must propel ourselves forward, especially when the obstacles and setbacks are frightening. At this point, you use the knowledge you have downloaded and hurl yourself forward to grab that next ring on the path to reaching dreams and goals.

I have always been inspired and motivated by entrepreneurs and understood the value they contribute to the world. The world needs more entrepreneurs to create new products, services, and jobs. My vision is to help aspiring and budding entrepreneurs change the world.

To pursue the dream of being an entrepreneur, I had to keep the vision and mission in front of my mind every day. Focusing on the image of the future and purpose propelled me forward and deterred thoughts of giving up. This was necessary to drive me toward each goal. One-step every day was like dipping my toe in the water.

Pride, fear, or thinking this is as good as life gets keep us in pain and stuck. When we repeat old patterns of thinking and acting, stop! Then grab this book and implement the information in the Shift, download, and propel chapters to get back on track. As you work on understanding thoughts, behaviors, and actions that derail dreams and goals.

You can anticipate and navigate those obstacles and setbacks to Keep Your Feet Moving.

PROPEL LESSONS LEARNED

1) Create a physical and digital vision board - include everything you want from your future list. Look at the board every day, several times a day to keep your mind focused on the dream

2) Approach someone living your dream - ask if you can help him or her or interview him or her

3) Seek support - join a support group, mastermind, or get an accountability coach to help you propel toward your dreams.

4) Stay focused on the vision - focus your gaze on what is ahead of you, only look back to carry the lessons learned so you will not make the same mistakes in the future.

Life is dynamic, robust, and sometimes despite our best efforts, we become overwhelmed and discouraged. If we remain open to new possibilities, willing to learn what we do not know, then we can work through challenges and setbacks.

PRACTICE PROPEL LESSONS LEARNED EXERCISE IN THE APPENDIX

"IF I HAD AN HOUR TO SOLVE A PROBLEM, I WOULD SPEND 55 MINUTES THINKING ABOUT THE PROBLEM AND 5 MINUTES THINKING ABOUT THE SOLUTION."
- ALBERT EINSTEIN

ENTREPRENEUR

[MERRIAM WEBSTER DICTIONARY]

ADJECTIVE

ENTREPRENEURIAL

ÄⁿN-TRƏ-P(R)Ə-ˈN(Y) U̇R-Ē-ƏL,-ˈNƏR-\

NOUN

ENTREPRENEURIALISM

ÄⁿN-TRƏ-P(R)Ə-ˈN(Y)U̇R-Ē-Ə-LI-ZƏM,-ˈNƏR-\

NOUN

ENTREPRENEURSHIP

ÄⁿN-TRƏ-P(R)Ə-ˈNƏR-ˌSHIP,-ˈN(Y)U̇R-\

One who organizes, manages, and assumes
the risk of a business or enterprise.

CHAPTER 8: WHAT IS AN ENTREPRENEUR?

I borrowed money from my retirement to fund my first business. The fear kept me up nights. I looked intensely at the patterns of life and quickly realized most of my decision-making was based on fear. The entrepreneur lives with the element of fear the product and business may fail.

Eric Reis, The Lean Startup's approach to managing uncertainty is to fail fast and learn quickly to improve the product and team. I surrendered the expectations of what life should look like and took the entrepreneurial journey.

Shifting from employee to business owner and then entrepreneur did not happen overnight. This transition took time and learning to the level of the fire hose.

According to Shaun "Shonduras" McBride, "An entrepreneur commands his emotions to fall in line and finds a way."

There are many definitions of an entrepreneur around the globe, and the meaning depends on whom you ask. Entrepreneurs are ordinary people that commit to tackling tough problems. The Entrepreneur of Things focuses on helping people use their experiences and skills to solve problems. We view entrepreneurship as a mindset and function in society to leverage the innovation economy.

We create products, provide services, and make improvements that solve problems. Those that take the entrepreneur path sometimes endure disbelief and isolation for not having a real job. The entrepreneur and team incur all the risk. One risk mitigation strategy is to keep increasing knowledge, asking for help, recognizing mistakes, and rejection are part of the process all while working 15-hour days, to improve the product and customer experience.

There were three main stages of growth before my mindset-transitioned from the seeker to the action-taker to that of a go-getter. Different mindsets and actions accompany each stage of growth. Each point in time requires a shift in mindset, relationships, and activities. To shift from one phase to the next, we let go of the past, download new information, take action, and propel toward our dreams.

Support was necessary for the decision to start a business, and my first step was to seek assistance from other entrepreneurs and business owners. When encountering new information, people, or situations that our background, education, culture, and experiences have no point of reference, we immediately reject the new person, place, or idea; instead of peeling back the layers of discovery.

I allocate time for learning and thinking about societal and business problems, working to build minimal viable products, securing clients, seeking feedback, and experimenting with different approaches. There are times progress explodes with success and other times incremental.

We are excited to work on the future possibilities around blockchain, artificial intelligence, biotechnology, and nanotechnology.

We all have the capability to think and function as an entrepreneur. This ongoing learning process requires collaboration, business, and financial literacy. The process takes time and work, but the rewards of nourishing your resiliency muscle and the knowledge gained will benefit your health, career, relationships, and business.

I do not have to go on this journey alone, and neither do you.

ENTREPRENEUR LESSONS LEARNED

1) Find the gap - identify where your experiences and instincts align with an opportunity to solve a societal or business problem.

2) Explore various problem-solving methods - There are many ways to approach a resolution each yielding diverse solutions based on the assumptions and questions you are trying to resolve.

3) Strategic partnerships - once you identify where you fit in the gap, research businesses, and entrepreneurs to connect and brainstorm to see if a synergistic collaboration is possible.

4) Do not operate in isolation - Locate companies and entrepreneurs that can help you build the bridge to your future.

5) Purge beliefs - If you are staying in your own world with people that think and look like you consider exploring your belief system about yours and others abilities and limitations.

6) Re-invent yourself - Never be afraid to change direction and reinvent yourself repeatedly. As the world cycles through change creativity, intuition, solving problems, and continually learning from diverse sources and people will help you and your business, identify new opportunities and avoid obsolescence.

Personal development in these areas will help you to transform from one economy to the next cycle.

PRACTICE ENTREPRENEUR LESSONS LEARNED EXERCISE IN THE APPENDIX

CYNDI MCCOY

CHAPTER 9: CONCLUSION

There comes a moment where the decision is made to let life push you around or pushback by moving past your situation and commanding emotions to fall in line. Deciding to work through setbacks and challenges increases self-esteem and provides real-life resiliency lessons.

When we are stuck, the natural progression to the next stage of life is interrupted. The inability to shift from beliefs that no longer serve you becomes debilitating to where people mentally are stuck in the old way of thinking, feeling, and acting. This mindset contributed to the perpetual loop of being unable to notice when circumstances and situations change or perceive solutions.

If you throw a diamond in the trash, does that make the diamond of less value?

The shift happens when we are ready to surrender and decide to do anything necessary to improve our situation. Commit to focusing on and appreciating what is in your hand and turn thinking toward possibilities.

The Shift, Download, and Propel plan is a bridge from one place to another. The same Shift, Download, and Propel roadmap will help a family navigate challenges to buying a house. This same structure will help a student obtain a college degree. The same process will help you grab that promotion. That same Shift, Download, and Propel blueprint will help you maneuver to adopt a healthier lifestyle.

The long walks helped me realize the same way leaves fall off trees during the winter, dry up, blow away and bloom bright green again in the spring. I too can flourish again and still have value.

The order and structure in Keep Your Feet Moving is flexible and open to adjustment when life signals it is time to change.

This framework is a bridge used whether you want to get a college degree, start a business, move up the career ladder, or adopt a wellness lifestyle.

Any age and stage where a major transformation is needed to grab fulfillment in life or business. Keep Your Feet Moving serves as an outline to ride the roller coaster of thoughts, relationships, and actions. For anyone desiring a different life, the boundaries, order, and structure are necessary to move through obstacles and setbacks that derail many dreams.

Keep Your Feet Moving provides a roadmap to reach your dreams by staying in action regardless of the challenge or setback.

I hope you will choose to come with me as we work through obstacles and find this book a helpful tool on your journey.

KEEP YOUR FEET MOVING AND NAVIGATE CHALLENGES ON THE ROAD TO ENTREPRENEURSHIP

APPENDIX

THE SHIFT LESSONS LEARNED EXERCISE

1. WHAT THREE THINGS ARE YOU MOST THANKFUL?

_____

_____

2. WHAT ARE YOUR CURRENT TALENTS AND SKILLS?

_____

_____

3. WHAT IS YOUR DREAM FOR THE FUTURE?

_____

_____

4. WHAT DO YOU NEED TO LEARN TO OBTAIN YOUR FUTURE?

_____

_____

MINDSET LESSONS LEARNED EXERCISE

1. DESCRIBE A SCENARIO WHERE YOU DISPLAYED THE GROWTH MINDSET.

_____

_____

2. DESCRIBE A SCENARIO WHERE YOU DISPLAYED THE FIXED MINDSET.

_____

_____

3. DO YOU BELIEVE THAT SUCCESSFUL PEOPLE HAVE ALL THE ANSWERS?

_____

_____

4. WHEN A CLOSE FRIEND SUGGESTS A FAVORITE RESTAURANT BUT YOU DO NOT LIKE THE FOOD, HOW DO YOU RESPOND AND WHY?

_____

RELATIONSHIP LESSONS LEARNED EXERCISE

1.WRITE THE NAMES OF THOSE THAT APPRECIATE AND SUPPORT YOUR FUTURE GOALS.

_____

_____

2. WHO WILL YOU SPEND LESS TIME WITH TO ACHIEVE YOUR GOALS?

_____

_____

3. WHOM DO YOU NEED TO FORGIVE TO RELEASE HURT FEELINGS AND MOVE INTO THE FUTURE?

_____

_____

ACTIONS LESSONS LEARNED EXERCISE

1. REVIEW YOUR DREAM FOR THE FUTURE AND WRITE DOWN THREE GOALS THAT WILL MOVE YOU CLOSER TO YOUR DREAM.

_____

_____

2. HOW WILL YOU USE THE LESSONS LEARNED TO STAY ON TRACK FOR YOUR GOALS?

_____

_____

3.SHARE A PAST OR CURRENT SITUATION WHERE YOUR ACTIONS SURPRISED YOU AND THOSE AROUND YOU.

_____

_____

4. WHAT WILL YOU DO EACH WEEK OUT OF YOUR COMFORT ZONE?

_____

PROPEL LESSONS LEARNED
EXERCISE

1. WHY DO YOU WANT THIS DREAM?

_____

_____

2. WHAT PICTURES DO YOU SEE WHEN YOU THINK OF THIS DREAM?

_____

_____

3.WHAT POWER THOUGHTS, WORDS, AFFIRMATIONS, AND ACTIONS WILL YOU USE TO STAY MOTIVATED TO ACHIEVE THIS DREAM?

_____

_____

4. WHAT ARE YOU PREPARED TO DO TO PUSH THROUGH TO ACHIEVE RESULTS?

_____

_____

ENTREPRENEUR LESSONS LEARNED EXERCISE

1. WHAT ARE YOU BUILDING?

---

2. DO YOU LOOK AT EXISTING PRODUCTS AND SERVICES AND THINK OF WAYS TO MAKE THEM BETTER?

---

3. WHAT PRODUCT OR SERVICE WILL YOU BUSINESS PROVIDE?

---

4. WHO ARE THE CUSTOMERS YOUR PRODUCT OR SERVICE WILL SERVE?

---

5. WHAT IS UNIQUE ABOUT YOUR PRODUCT OR SERVICE THAT WILL COMPEL CUSTOMERS TO BUY?

---

6. HOW MUCH MONEY DO YOU NEED FOR YOUR BUSINESS?

GOALS

1ST QUARTER GOALS

_____

_____

CRITERIA FOR SUCCESS
HOW WILL YOU MEASURE?

_____

2ND QUARTER GOALS

_____

_____

CRITERIA FOR SUCCESS
HOW WILL YOU MEASURE?

_____

3RD QUARTER GOALS

_____

_____

CRITERIA FOR SUCCESS
HOW WILL YOU MEASURE?

_____

4TH QUARTER GOALS

_____

_____

CRITERIA FOR SUCCESS
HOW WILL YOU MEASURE?

_____

KEEP YOUR FEET MOVING AND NAVIGATE CHALLENGES ON THE ROAD TO ENTREPRENEURSHIP

JOURNAL PRACTICE

VISION BOARD

ENDNOTES

Opening
Oprah Windfrey,
www.oprah.com/quote/oprah-quote-on-reaching

Chapter 2
Dr. Joe Dispenza, Breaking the Habit of Being Yourself
Nelson Mandela,
www.good.reads.com/quotes/956662-may-your-choices-reflect-your-hopes-not-your-fears
Merriam Webster Dictionary, www.merriam-webster.com
Tim Roth, Strengthsfinder 2.0

Chapter 3
Sloan Asynchronous Learning Network,
onlinelearningconsortium.org/about/history
T.D. Jakes, Reposition Yourself, Living Life Without Limits
Dr.Carol Dweck, Mindset; The New Psychology of Success
Andrew McAfee, and Erik Brynjolfsson, Machine, Platform, Crowd
Dr. Mercola, Effortless Healing

Chapter 4
Mahatma Gandhi,
www.goodreads.com/quotes/50584-your-beliefs-become-your-thoughts-your-thoughts-your-thoughts-become-your-words

Chapter 5
Dr.Carol Dweck, Mindset; The New Psychology of Success
Swami Rami, The Science of Breath
Dr. Van Moody, the People Factor

Chapter 6
Dr. Van Moody, the People Factor
Psychology Today,
www.psychologytoday.com/us/topics/relationships

Chapter 7
Vishen Lakahani, Code of The Extraordinary mind
Dr. Mercola,
Emotional Freedom Technique, eft.mercola.com

Chapter 8
The American Ninja Warrior ™ TV show
en.wikipedia.org/wiki/American Ninja Warrior

Chapter 9
Eric Reis, The Lean Startup
Shaun"Shonduras"Mcbride,
www.forbes.com/profile/shaun-mcbride/#66320c235929

ABOUT THE AUTHOR

Cyndi is the founder of the D-COM Corporation, a company that provides products and services for start-ups and Fortune 500 companies in the Financial Services, Government, Healthcare, Information Technology, and Retail industries.

She is a catalyst with the primary goal of helping people and businesses transform to participate in the innovation economy. Cyndi understands the value entrepreneurs contribute to the world. She started The Entrepreneur of Things to unleash entrepreneurial energy and provide support to aspiring and budding entrepreneurs.